Microwave Ovens

Cristie Reed

Rourke
educational Media

rkeeducationalmedia.com

Scan for Related Titles
and Teacher Resources

Teaching Focus:
Concepts of Print- Have students find capital letters and punctuation in a sentence. Ask students to explain the purpose for using them in a sentence.

Before Reading:

Building Academic Vocabulary and Background Knowledge

Before reading a book, it is important to set the stage for your child or student by using pre-reading strategies. This will help them develop their vocabulary, increase their reading comprehension, and make connections across the curriculum.

1. *Read the title and look at the cover. Let's make predictions about what this book will be about.*
2. *Take a picture walk by talking about the pictures/photographs in the book. Implant the vocabulary as you take the picture walk. Be sure to talk about the text features such as headings, Table of Contents, glossary, bolded words, captions, charts/ diagrams, or Index.*
3. Have students read the first page of text with you then have students read the remaining text.
4. *Strategy Talk – use to assist students while reading.*
   - *Get your mouth ready*
   - *Look at the picture*
   - *Think…does it make sense*
   - *Think…does it look right*
   - *Think…does it sound right*
   - *Chunk it – by looking for a part you know*
5. *Read it again.*
6. *After reading the book complete the activities below.*

Content Area Vocabulary
Use glossary words in a sentence.

absorb
appliance
conventional
energy
molecules
radio waves

After Reading:

Comprehension and Extension Activity

After reading the book, work on the following questions with your child or students in order to check their level of reading comprehension and content mastery.

1. *How do molecules affect the temperature of food? (Asking questions)*
2. *Why are microwave ovens helpful to families? (Connecting text to self)*
3. *What are radio waves? (Summarize)*
4. *What are some differences between conventional ovens and microwave ovens? (Summarize)*

Extension Activity

Look in your freezer for packaged foods such as burritos, vegetables, pizzas, or other meals. Choose one item and look at the cooking directions. What are some ways the product can be cooked? What are the differences in prepping the food between the conventional oven and microwave oven? What are the cooking time differences? Which method would be best if you are running late for school or practice?

Table of Contents

Cooking Gets Easier 4

How Microwave Ovens Cook Food 8

Microwave Cooking 18

Photo Glossary 22

Index 24

Websites to Visit 24

About the Author 24

Cooking Gets Easier

Microwave ovens save time and effort in the kitchen. They cook food quickly and with little mess. They are easy to use. They are small enough to fit into any kitchen space and they save **energy**.

Before the 1970s, the kitchen stove was the main **appliance** used for cooking. But once microwaves came into our kitchens, **conventional** ways of cooking started to change!

In 1950, an engineer named Percy Spencer was experimenting with electricity when a chocolate bar melted in his pocket. Spencer realized his device could be used to heat food. His mistake led to the invention of the microwave oven!

Spencer's first microwave oven was about 5 feet (1.5 meters) high.

How Microwave Ovens Cook Food

Your microwave oven gets its name from the special kind of **radio waves** it creates. The waves travel very fast.

Microwaves can be dangerous to humans. Microwave ovens are covered by strong metal boxes so no waves can escape.

The inside of the oven is metal. The microwaves bounce back and forth off the metal walls.

microwaves

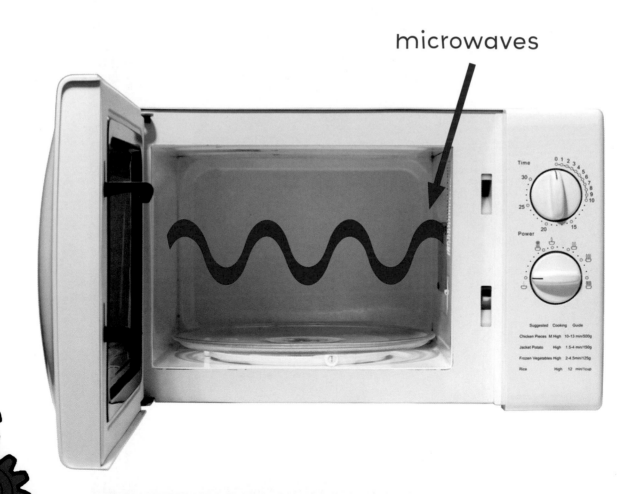

Inside every microwave oven is a special device called a magnetron. This device creates the microwaves that cook your food.

magnetron

Food is placed on a turntable. It moves slowly around the oven. This helps make sure the food is heated evenly.

turntable

Microwaves are unique. Water, fats, and sugars in foods **absorb** microwaves. Microwaves are not absorbed by most plastic or glass. Metal reflects, or blocks, microwaves.

Food can be cooked in glass, plastic, paper, or ceramic containers. Never put metal inside a microwave!

When microwaves enter food, they cause the food **molecules** to move. This movement creates heat. The more the molecules move, the hotter the food gets.

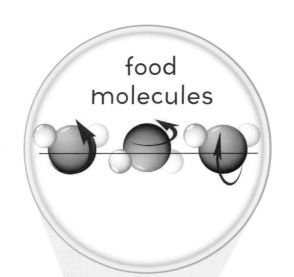

food
molecules

Microwave Cooking

Conventional ovens cook food with hot, dry air. Microwave ovens use waves, so the air does not get hot.

In conventional ovens, heat moves from the outside of food to the middle. Microwave ovens cook food everywhere all at once.

In regular ovens heat moves from the oven to the food.

Conventional ovens and stoves help us make great tasting food. Microwave ovens help us when we want to save time in the kitchen.

So, next time you need a quick snack, put in some popcorn and set the timer. You'll be enjoying a tasty treat in no time!

Photo Glossary

 **absorb** (ab-ZORB): To soak up.

 **appliance** (uh-PLYE-uhnss): A machine designed to do a job.

 **conventional** (kuhn-VEN-shuh-nuhl): To do things in an accepted way.

 **energy** (EN-ur-gee): Power from electricity.

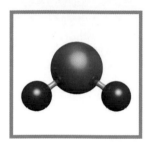 **molecules** (MOL-uh-kyools): The smallest part of a substance made of one or more atoms.

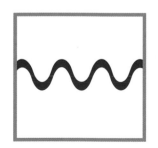 **radio waves** (RAY-dee-oh wayvz): Invisible electromagnetic waves.

Index

appliance 6

cook 4, 11, 18

food(s) 4, 7, 11, 12, 15,
   16, 18, 20

heat 7, 16, 18, 19

magnetron 11

metal 8, 10, 14, 15

microwaves 6, 8, 10, 11,
   14, 16

molecules 16

ovens 4, 8, 18, 19, 20

radio waves 8

Websites to Visit

www.lawrencehallofscience.org/kidsite

www.sciencekids.co.nz/physics.html

www.tryscience.org/home

Meet The Author!
www.meetREMauthors.com

About the Author

Cristie Reed has been a teacher for many years. She specializes in teaching reading to kids. She loves to learn about new things, including the latest technology and gadgets. She knows kids are naturally curious about how things work. She hopes that through reading, kids can find answers to their most important questions.

www.rourkeeducationalmedia.com

PHOTO CREDITS: Cover © Mazz-Studio; title page, 21 © impactimage; page 5, 22, 23 © MAFord; page 6 © Everett Collection; page 7 © Acroterion; page 8 © Rostislav Sedlacek; page 10 © 2happy; page 11, 22 © Designya; page 13 © Spauln; page 15 © watin klaisuk, Mrsiraphol, Lane V. Erickson, Iakov Filimonor; page 17 © designua; pae 19, 22 © Yin Yang; page 20 © desertsolitare

Edited by: Jill Sherman

Cover by: Nicola Stratford, nicolastratford.com
Interior design by: Jen Thomas

Library of Congress PCN Data

Microwave Ovens/ Cristie Reed
   (How It Works)
   ISBN (hard cover)(alk. paper) 978-1-62717-646-0
   ISBN (soft cover) 978-1-62717-768-9
   ISBN (e-Book) 978-1-62717-888-4
   Library of Congress Control Number: 2014934238
   Printed in the United States of America, North Mankato, Minnesota

Also Available as: